Steadfast

AN INDUCTIVE BIBLE STUDY
ON 1 & 2 PETER

By
Erin H. Warren

contents

start here

I sat excitedly in my chair in the school library. It was character award day, and I couldn't wait to find out what my teacher saw in me. I sat patiently waiting my turn. Okay, not-so-patiently. *That* wouldn't be my award, but I had high hopes. I listened as the other girls in my class were called and praised for *their* patience, joy, love, kindness—all the sweet things. I wanted an award for a sweet trait too.

Finally, she called my name. "Erin Headley, steadfast."

I'm sorry. What?! Steadfast?! Not joy? Surely, I was joyful? What about encouraging? That worked well "Encouraging Erin." But steadfast?

I was not thrilled. Truth be told, I didn't even know what the word meant. Of all the traits, why did I get the one that I didn't even know what it meant?! Afterward, I stood in a small circle of classmates, letting my disappointment be known. I have this vivid memory of flipping my hand holding the certificate and exclaiming, "I don't even know what this means!" That's when one of the boys in my class chimed in, "It means you're stubborn."

Oh, that's when I lost it. *Stubborn? I won the stubborn award?!*

We often think of steadfastness as a negative trait. It's the nicer way we try to describe a hard-headed person or difficult, opinionated child. *She is so steadfast!* What we really mean is *She is so hard to change! She doesn't compromise! She is unyielding and obstinate!*

Being steadfast isn't a negative. I know because steadfast describes our God. It would take me years to recognize the gift of steadfastness and fully understand what an incredible character trait it is. But here's the thing about steadfastness: it's only profitable when it is applied to the right areas of our life. Take each of those statements and think of them in context of your faith. What if we were so rooted in truth that no matter what happened to us, we remained steadfast in our faith? Could it be said of us that we do not compromise what we believe? Are we unyielding in following Jesus? Do we continue to persevere in worship and obedience, even when life around us is hard?

Merriam-Webster defines *steadfast* as "firmly fixed in place: Immovable."[1] And that is the call of 1 and 2 Peter: to stand firm in our faith no matter what comes our way—to remain fixed, to stay the course, to keep pursuing Jesus. We are called to be steadfast.

---

1   "Steadfast." *Merriam-Webster.com Dictionary*, Merriam-Webster, https://www.merriam-webster.com/dictionary/steadfast. Accessed 3 Jun. 2024.)

My life does not look at all like I thought it would. Some things are better than I could have imagined, but I've also walked through some faith-rocking hardships over the last decade. I am going to guess you could probably say the same thing of your own life. Suffering here is inevitable; it's part of life in a broken world (John 16:33). But steadfastness helps protect us when our world falls apart. The decision to cling to faith, to cling to truth, to cling to God Himself even amid pain, tears, sadness, and hardship, is where we find hope. And not just any hope; Peter calls it "living hope" (1 Peter 1:3).

Our theme verse for this study is one that brings tears to my eyes every time I read it.

> *Once you were not a people, but now you are God's people; once you had not*
> *received mercy, but now you have received mercy.*
> *1 Peter 2:10*

You may be wondering what the connection is between the title of the study and the theme verse. What does being steadfast have to do with being God's people and receiving His mercy? Our temptation with books like 1 and 2 Peter is to fall into the trap of obeying out of our own strength. A great deal of these verses speak to how we should act and live because we are part of God's family, and we can sometimes get wrapped up in what we should do and separate it from the Source of our obedience. As I often say, "Obedience is not an obligation; it's an overflow."[1] We can *only* remain steadfast in faith and obey His commands because we are His and His power is in us. When we begin to grasp how glorious and powerful our God is, then we will find ourselves utterly humbled to be God's people and receive His mercy. The overflow of that should be a life marked by steadfast faith.

As I have studied Scripture and steadfastness more, I have come to understand the beauty of this character trait. I now see how my God-given steadfastness has served me well through many seasons of life. Steadfastness is what keeps you from compromise, protects your actions when your feelings waver, and holds you in place when the circumstances of life toss you to-and-fro.

But what I love most about steadfastness is that it describes our God. He's immovable, fixed, unchanging (the fancy word for it is *immutable*). He's the same yesterday, today, tomorrow, and forevermore (Hebrews 13:8). Because He is steadfast, we can steadfastly stand firm in our faith, trust that His Word is true, and remain anchored in a living hope that eternity is real.

A LITTLE BACKGROUND INFORMATION

Both 1 and 2 Peter were letters written by Peter (or Simon Peter as he is sometimes called in Scripture), one of Jesus' closest disciples, and he wrote to mostly Gentile believers in Asia Minor (which is modern day Turkey). The two letters were written several years apart, but both were written while Peter was in Rome and both during a time of growing persecution in the church. It was about thirty years after the resurrection of Jesus, and Nero was emperor over the Roman Empire. He was notorious for his persecution of Christians, but for these believers in "Pontus,

---

1   Warren, Erin H. *Feasting on Truth: Savor the Life-Giving Word of God.* Orlando, FL, Headley Warren Productions LLC, 15 Dec. 2022, p. 140.

Galatia, Cappadocia, Asia, and Bithynia" (1 Peter 1:1), the Greco-Roman society they lived in was becoming increasingly hostile toward them and their faith.

In the face of spreading persecution and hardship, Peter wrote his first letter to encourage these believers. He wanted them to know they were not alone, to give them hope for the future, and to stand firm in what they knew to be true. Based on Peter's words in these letters, we can guess that many may have been questioning their faith. *Is this Jesus true? Is eternity real? How do I reconcile suffering and faith? How do I live obediently in the face of persecution?*

Some of my favorite passages in Scripture are found in 1 Peter, and many of them have been a source of encouragement as I have walked through my own faith-refining fires.

Peter's tone in his second letter intensified the call to steadfastness as another threat to Christianity spread: false teaching. Here, Peter gave practical responses to the objections of the culture around them and encouraged Christians to a steadfast pursuit of truth and knowledge. This second letter was written near the end of Peter's life, and his purpose was to give a written account of his teaching that would outlast his own life. I love that two-thousand years later, we are still studying and applying his encouragement.

As one of Jesus' closest disciples, Peter was an *eyewitness* to Jesus's life. *This* is what I love most about Peter's letters! There are so many direct connections to events in the gospels and quotes from Jesus, so we will be cross-referencing to the gospels frequently throughout the study. But even more so, Peter also referenced the Old Testament quite a bit, which is fascinating given his original audience (and great hope for us today too).

IMPORTANT: Cultural context is important when studying Scripture. We must remember that while the Bible was written for us, it was not written to us. That's not to say the meaning changes with culture, but that we must first understand what these passages meant to the original audience. Only then can we better understand and apply the truths to our lives today. There are several passages in these letters that will require some deeper study of the cultural context, particularly on the topics of slaves and women. To better understand these passages, I highly recommend consulting a trusted cultural commentary. You can find several recommended resources on my website: FeastingOnTruth.com/Resources.

WHY STUDY INDUCTIVELY?

This study is designed to provide a foundation for inductive Bible study. When I first heard of inductive study, I was pretty intimidated. But, it's just a fancy term for studying with your own heart and mind first. I honestly didn't even know I *could* study this way until a few years ago at a conference. I had the privilege of hearing one of my favorite Bible teachers speak, and the following quote from her talk forever changed the way I look at Bible study:

> *We cannot be content being curators of other people's opinions about a book we*
> *can't be bothered to read ourselves.* — Jen Wilkin

I realized my entire Christian life I had been a librarian, curating other people's thoughts and beliefs and study findings. It became my driving passion to not only read and study Scripture for myself, but to help other women do the same. I'm so glad you're here! My prayer is that this book helps you:

- Release the bonds of a "perfect quiet time" to find deeper, richer time in the Word
- Build confidence as you learn how to study the Bible firsthand
- Discover truths about God and His character
- Connect the Old and New Testaments
- Grow in your faith and knowledge in a way that produces life change

HOW TO USE THIS STUDY

Feasting on Truth has several levels of studies, and I classify this one as True Inductive. We will use four simple questions (see page 11) to guide our study. Each week will focus on one chapter, and you'll see that the homework includes a guide through those four questions. Under *What Does This Mean?* you'll see some suggested words to look up in the dictionary as well as space to write cross-references (other verses that speak to the same topic or help explain the meaning). There are also a few questions to help kick-start your study but won't cover everything. These are intended to help get you thinking on your own and are not all-inclusive of the meaning. Each week also includes two blank pages for you to make your own notes. I purposely left this section wide open for you, or rather for the Holy Spirit. I want you to have the freedom to take notes in the format you choose: write out specific verses, record observations, make a chart, rewrite commentary quotes or Greek definitions, etc. Each week also includes pages for teaching notes and group notes. I know it can sound intimidating, but I also know you can do it!

Studying a chapter a week is my favorite way to study. I encourage you to read each chapter (and listen to it on your favorite Bible app) over and over throughout the week, then pick a day or two to focus on studying. Always, always start with prayer. Ask the Holy Spirit to guide you in your study time and to reveal truth to you. It's His job (John 14:26; 16:13–15). You'll be amazed at what the Holy Spirit can teach when you give Him the space to speak.

Teaching for each chapter is available on Season 11 of the Feasting on Truth Podcast or my YouTube channel: www.FeastingOnTruth.com/c/erinhwarren.

Here are some more tips to help you as you study:

Move Slowly

Many Bible studies plow through Scripture, covering a chapter (or sometimes more) a day. There's certainly a time and a place for that, but I've found when I move through Scripture slowly, reading small sections or focusing on one aspect of the study over the course of one week, the Word of God soaks into my heart and mind deeply. I remember it more easily. I memorize it more effectively. What I love about this particular way of studying is that if I feel the need to stop and let a particular verse sink in, I can do so without feeling like I'm falling behind. It also leaves room for the Holy Spirit to do what only He can do. Which leads me to . . .

Let the Holy Spirit Guide You

Jesus gives us this promise in John 14:26: "But the Helper, the Holy Spirit, whom the Father will send in my name, he will teach you all things and bring to your remembrance all that I have said to you." Anytime I sit down to study, I start with prayer. I ask the Holy Spirit to teach me all the things and to help me remember all the things. That's His job. He's there to help, so invite Him into your time.

Take the Pressure Off

Our time with the Lord doesn't have to be this picture-perfect composition of Bible, notebook, and a cup of coffee (oh how I do love me some good coffee though). The words "quiet time" are not in the Bible, and I've found one size does not fit all. Our time in the Word will change with our stage of life. I tend to deep-dive study about twice a week, but I meditate on it every day. You may sit down and do all of your study in one day or you may devote an hour a day. Find what works for you and stick with it!

Don't Do This Alone

Some of my deepest relationships are ones built on the Word. They are women who gathered around a table or in a living room or online, and we had hard conversations with the Word of Truth between us. Invite a few girlfriends to do this with you. I even included a fun recipe in the back of the book you can make when you get together!

I recommend completing all of the homework on your own before listening to the teaching for the week. You can either listen on your own time or watch together with your group.

Finding time is hard. Women often tell me that they need to put their families first, that work is too crazy, or that they just don't have time to get together with other women for Bible study. Can I challenge you a bit? Is there any time more well spent than investing in our relationship with God? It's hard to pour out from an empty cup. We need to be constantly filled with Jesus, so we can pour out Jesus to our friends, family, and to God. Yes, this may look different in different seasons of life, but you won't regret making it a priority to spend time in the Word with other women.

COMPANION TEACHINGS AND OTHER RESOURCES

I am committed to walking alongside you as you study Scripture inductively. I know you can do this, and I want to help you be successful. I have personally curated and put together a valuable study resource for you called *The Alongside Guide*. Each week, you'll receive an email from me with helpful insight, links to that week's teaching video and podcast, study notes with cross-references, quotes, characteristics of God, small group discussion questions, and more. It's everything you need to be successful in your study, and it gets delivered right to your inbox. Scan the QR code or visit FeastingOnTruth.com/Peter to sign up.

LET'S FEAST

The word *feast* is rooted in abundance, and that's what awaits us in Scripture: a table laid out before us, not only for our essential nourishment, but also for our enjoyment. It is my prayer that the Holy Spirit meets you in the pages of 1 and 2 Peter, and that through this study you will be empowered to stand firm and steadfast in faith. And not because you are strong, but because you know beyond a shadow of a doubt who your God is and what He did for you!

I am cheering for you! Happy feasting!

Because of Christ,

Erin H. Warren

four simple questions

Good Bible study is rooted in asking the right questions of Scripture. Our first inclination in Bible study is often to ask, "What does this mean to me?" We want to cut right to the ending. Instead, learning to first understand the context, summary, and character of God in the passage will help us better discern the meaning and our response. I have adopted what I call *Four Simple Questions* as the foundation of my time in the Word. Yes, this takes a little more time and effort, but the practice of persevering through the Word is a valuable one. These four simple questions, as well as other helpful tips and resources for inductive study, are further explained in my book, *Feasting on Truth: Savor the Life-giving Word of God.*

START WITH CONTEXT

It's important to remember that while the Bible was written for us and is applicable to our lives today (Hebrews 4:12), we are not the original audience. It is a book not written in modern America, but in the ancient Middle East. If we do not first answer some key questions to understand the context, we cannot properly understand the passage and its intent. Most of these answers can be found in a good study Bible.

FOUR SIMPLE QUESTIONS

I realized that one of my downfalls when attempting to read and study the Bible for myself was not knowing which questions to ask. Many of the methods I tried were either too open or too rigid. Asking four simple questions provided the right balance of structure and flexibility I needed. I want to release you from thinking this has to look a certain way—it doesn't. Basically: Are you showing up? Are you changing? Are you connected? Does that make you want to keep showing up? If you answer yes to all of these, then you're on the right track! Here is a brief overview of each question:

1. **What does this say?**

   Before we can interpret Scripture, we need to know what's going on in the passage. Some methods would call this *observation* or the *aim of the passage*.

   - Write a 1–2 sentence summary of what the passage is about—no interpretation, just the facts.

   - Answer the questions: Who? What? Where? When?

   - Are there any repeated words or phrases?

   - Are there any transitional words (therefore, so, but, and, etc.)? Remember, every word is there for a reason.

2. **What does this say about God?**

   This to me has been the most transformative question to ask during Bible study. This book is not about us; it's about God. His character and name are written on every page. Before we can understand our response, we must know who He is.

   - What names of God are used? (His names speak to His character.)

   - What characteristics of God are in this passage?

   - I include Jesus in this as well: What does this passage tell us about Jesus?

   - You can find lists of the names and characteristics of God on pages 18–19.

   - Each week, complete the sentence "Because God is _____, I can _____."

3. **What does this mean?**

   PRAY. PRAY. PRAY. Ask the Holy Spirit to guide you in this. Using context, the summary, and other observations you have made, begin to be a detective. Remember the lens through which you are looking. Yes, this takes work, but it's worth doing!

   - Read the passage in multiple translations. What differences do you see?

   - Look up words in the English dictionary.

   - What other passages in Scripture are related to this one? (These are called cross-references.)

   - Read a trusted commentary or study Bible.

   - Research the original language (the Old Testament was originally written in Hebrew and the New Testament in Greek).

   - Go to FeastingOnTruth.com/Resources for recommended resources, Bibles, and commentaries.

4. **How should I respond?**

   Our Bible study should change us. John 17:17 says, "Sanctify them in the truth; your word is truth." *Sanctify* is a big churchy word that means "to purify or to make holy." It's the act of separating ourselves from the actions of our flesh and dedicating more of our lives and actions to God. God's Word has a purpose in our lives (Isaiah 55:10–11), and we shouldn't stop at knowing its meaning. Instead, we should respond:

   - Is there an action I need to take?

- A conversation I need to have?

- A moment of worship?

- Something I should let go?

- Write out a prayer.

However you feel led to respond, write it down and enlist someone to hold you accountable.

OTHER HELPFUL TIPS

Listen to the Passage

Use a Bible app to listen to the passages each week. We often feel like this is a cop-out, but for thousands of years, the Word of God was passed down orally from generation to generation. It's a book meant to be read out loud, and when you listen to it, you'll be amazed at how much you pick up on that you didn't notice when reading it.

Use Different Colored Pens

I've found using different colored pens when writing my study notes helps me remember where the note came from. For instance, I use different colors for rewriting the Scripture verses, my thoughts, certain study Bibles, cross-references or different translations, commentary quotes, and Greek or Hebrew word definitions. I don't really have a color system, so the colors change from time to time. That's okay too!

Start with a Clean Copy of God's Word

A study Bible adds additional commentary. Using a Bible that doesn't have any additional commentary removes the temptation to peek at notes before fully understanding the passage on your own. If you do not have a non-study Bible, don't fret! You can print out chapters on several Bible websites including www.BibleGateway.com. I use an ESV journaling Bible for my initial study (which has very few footnotes), then move to other translations and other study Bibles as I go through my study week. Speaking of translations . . .

A Note About Translations

There are a myriad of translations out there, so how do you know which to pick? First, it's important to know where translations come from. The Old Testament was originally written in Hebrew, while the New Testament was written in Greek (though a few portions of Scripture were written in Aramaic).

Over the years, translators have used original copies written in these languages to interpret Scripture into English (and other languages as well). Translations fall on a spectrum between two ends: word-for-word (translations that use the closest English word to the original word) and thought-for-thought (translations that rephrase the words into more modern, understandable English). Technically, all of them are a mix of the two, but some lean more toward one end or the other.

Some examples of translations that lean toward word-for-word include: English Standard Version (ESV—my top choice), New American Standard Bible (NAS or NASB), and King James Version (KJV). These are the closest to the original language, but we can sometimes miss the cultural context.

An example of thought-for-thought is the New Living Translation (NLT).

There are also versions that are more toward the middle of the spectrum, such as the Christian Standard Bible (CSB) and the New International Version (NIV).

The last kind of translation is not necessarily a translation at all, but rather a paraphrase. Paraphrase Bibles, like *The Message*, should be treated more like commentary because, while they can bring insight into the meaning of the passage, they are not Scripture themselves. I rarely use this type. If you do use a paraphrase, wait until you've completed questions 1–3 and are consulting other commentaries for additional insights.

Welcome to the Feast!

See? Simple. Yes, it takes practice, but honestly, it doesn't take as long as you'd think. You just have to be willing to spend time with Jesus. In Acts 4, Peter and John are on trial before the religious leaders (the smartest of the smart when it came to the Law), and in verse 13 it says, "Now when they saw the boldness of Peter and John, and perceived that they were uneducated, common men, they were astonished. And they recognized that they had been with Jesus." Uneducated. Common. Peter and John hadn't been to seminary, but they had been *with* Jesus.

What I've found is that there is not one method that will make all of this work for you. The power is not in the method. The power is in the Word of God. The power is in spending time with Jesus in the Word with the Holy Spirit as your guide.

When you see your life change and you find community around the Word, you will find yourself returning to Scripture, growing more confident as you study, and discovering the joy and excitement of Feasting on Truth.

Visit FeastingOnTruth.com/HowTo for more information
and in-depth teachings on these questions.

small group guide

am a firm believer in gathering together around the Word of God. It is at the heart of Feasting on Truth. As stated in *start here*, I believe that small group discussion is incredibly important when studying the Bible. I heard a pastor say, "Our time in the Word should be personal but never private." I do not believe we are called to study in isolation, I believe it is in places of isolation where Satan loves to tempt us. Discussing the passage in a small group setting (even if it's with only one other woman) helps confirm what the Holy Spirit taught us. It holds us accountable to truth. Not only that, but I learn so much from other women too. They will see truths within those passages that I miss. It helps build layers of understanding.

Leading a group is not nearly as difficult as it seems. I like to think of group leaders more like discussion leaders. A great discussion leader talks less than a third of the group time. You may need to speak first or jump in to get the conversation going, but the goal is to get the group talking.

Here are some other tips and a guide for your small group time:

Lead with authenticity
You do not have to have all the answers or have it all together to lead. I do not have it all together, and I fail miserably every day at doing what I know I should (Romans 7!). But I don't have to air all my dirty laundry to be authentic, and I never want my authenticity to enable sin in other people's lives. I've found that when I'm real about where I am and I invite women in to see how God is working on me in those areas, it invites them into authentic life change as well.

Set up a group text or use a group chat app
Connection throughout the week is key to building connection within your group. If you are not tech savvy or keeping up with a group chat isn't your strength, ask someone in the group to take charge of that. It's a great way to get others involved too! Throughout the week, you can check in on your group or share a verse or a particular insight into the passage.

Start with an ice breaker question
It doesn't have to be deep or spiritual, just something to get the conversation flowing. These types of questions are always a great way to help a group of women get to know each other.

Share your summary

Have the women share their summary for that week's passage. Depending on the size of your group, you may want to limit this to two to three women.

Ask: What characteristics of God did you see in this week's passage?

This works well "popcorn style." Let the women jump in with various names and characteristics of God and the verses that correspond. I usually add these to my own notes as well.

Use the weekly discussion questions

There are discussion questions marked within each week's homework. For additional weekly discussion questions, go to FeastingOnTruth.com/Peter and sign up to receive *The Alongside Guide* in your email. Each week, you'll get additional questions (as well as other resources and notes) delivered right to your inbox.

Share "Because God is" statements

This is a simple one, and I love it when everyone shares theirs! Depending on how long you have been together, some women in your group may not feel comfortable sharing the nitty-gritty of their lives. Having everyone share their "Because God is" statement is a way to engage the women who do not feel comfortable speaking up.

Share prayer requests

Sharing what is going on in our lives opens the door to build community and meet needs. I'll never forget sitting in a group when a woman shared that she needed prayer that she could pass her driving test. Across the table, another woman in the group spoke up and said, "I can help you learn to drive!" A couple months later, I received a picture of the two women holding a brand-new driver's license. It was incredible! Praying for one another is commanded, so allow time for this with your group. Pray with one another. Pray throughout the week. When we do this, we get to share an inheritance in what God is doing through the lives of others.

GROUP LIST

NAME	PHONE	EMAIL

knowing God

For too many years, I struggled with knowing how to interpret Scripture and apply these ancient words to my life. I did not know that God promises to equip us in studying Scripture through the Holy Spirit. And truthfully, I treated my Bible like one of those balls you shake, ask a question, flip over, and find your answer. Too many times I came to Scripture looking for an answer to my question, or I treated it like a yearbook—looking for all the pictures of myself.

Then, I began asking a different question, and my entire Bible study and life changed. I asked, "What does this say about God?" This shifted my perspective from a self-centered approach toward Scripture (where I am always asking, "What does this mean *to* me or *for* me?") to a God-centered approach—intentionally looking for and seeking out what each passage teaches me about God.

The Bible is not about me. It is first and foremost a book about God, and His name and character are written across every page. Our purpose on earth is to know God and make Him known, to love God and love others. But we can't love what we don't know; we can't worship what we don't know. And the primary way we know God is through His Word. The pursuit of knowledge about God is not optional; it's essential.

On the following pages, you will find two lists to help you: Names of God and Characteristics of God. It's not comprehensive, and there are spaces for you to add others as you discover more with each passage you read. Here are ways you can have a God-centered approach to your study:

- Ask, "What characteristics of God do I see in this passage?"

- Ask, "What names of God do I see in this passage?" (His names speak to His character.)

- Complete this sentence: Because God is _____, I can _____.

While there are different roles within the Trinity (God the Father, God the Son, and God the Holy Spirit), for the sake of simplicity, I study them as One. If you need further help, visit www.FeastingOnTruth.com for more information and resources.

names of God

Abba Father

Adonai *(Lord, Master)*

Alpha and Omega

Bread of Life

Chief Cornerstone

Creator

Deliverer

El Elyon *(The Most High God)*

El Olam *(The Everlasting God)*

El Roi *(The God Who Sees Me)*

El Shaddai *(The Lord God Almighty)*

Elohim

Everlasting Father

Great High Priest

Holy One

I AM

Immanuel

King of Kings

Lamb of God

Light of the World

Lion of Judah

Lord of Lords

Mighty God

Morning Star

Prince of Peace

Resurrection and the Life

Savior

Wonderful Counselor

Yahweh Amen *(The Lord is Truth)*

Yahweh Jireh *(The Lord Provides)*

Yahweh Nissi *(The Lord is my Banner)*

Yahweh-Raah *(The Lord is my Shepherd)*

Yahweh Rapha *(The Lord Heals)*

Yahweh Shalom *(The Lord is Peace)*

characteristics of God

Abounding in Steadfast Love

Compassionate

Deliberate

Faithful

Forgiving

Full of Grace

Good

Glorious

Gracious

Guide

Holy

Immutable *(Unchanging)*

Infinite

Invisible

Jealous

Just

Kind

Long-Suffering/Patient

Love

Merciful

Mighty

Omnipotent *(All-Powerful)*

Omnipresent

Omniscient *(All-Knowing)*

One

Perfect

Protector

Provider

Refuge/Help

Righteous

Self-Sufficient

Slow to Anger

Sovereign

Trustworthy

Truth

Wise

With Us

Steadfast

KNOWING GOD NOTES

Steadfast

CONTEXT

Steadfast

CONTEXT NOTES

Who wrote 1 and 2 Peter?

What do you know about this author?

To whom were these books written?

When were they written?

What is the genre of these books?

What was the intent or purpose?

What was going on in history when each of them were written?

Steadfast

CONTEXT NOTES

Steadfast

CONTEXT NOTES

Steadfast

TEACHING NOTES

Steadfast

TEACHING NOTES

Steadfast

GROUP NOTES

Steadfast

GROUP NOTES

Steadfast

1 PETER 1

Steadfast

1 PETER 1 NOTES

READ 1 PETER 1

WHAT DOES THIS SAY?

Write a 2–3 sentence summary of this passage.

Who? What? Where? When?

List any repeated words or phrases.

List any transitional words.

Steadfast

1 PETER 1 NOTES

WHAT DOES THIS SAY ABOUT GOD?

What characteristics of God do you see in this passage?

WHAT DOES THIS MEAN?

Look up the following words in the dictionary and write out their definitions:

Imperishable:

Holy:

_____:

_____:

Steadfast

1 PETER 1 NOTES

CROSS-REFERENCES

Isaiah 40:6–8:

Hebrews 10:19–39:

_____:

_____:

_____:

STARTER QUESTIONS

How does Peter describe our inheritance? Why would this be encouraging to the original audience?

According to this passage, what three things play a role in our sanctification or purification?

Steadfast

DISCUSSION: Revisit the context information about Peter. How does Peter's past as it relates to grief and suffering shape his message in this passage?

DISCUSSION: How do these Old Testament passages help explain Peter's message in this chapter?

Leviticus 11:44–45:

Exodus 12:1–28:

Jeremiah 31:31–40:

DISCUSSION: What are we called to in light of our salvation?

Steadfast

1 PETER 1 NOTES

Steadfast

1 PETER 1 NOTES

Steadfast

HOW SHOULD I RESPOND?

How is God steadfast in this chapter? How does this help you remain steadfast in faith?

Write a prayer of thanksgiving for who He is.

Because God is:

    I can:

Steadfast

TEACHING NOTES

Steadfast

TEACHING NOTES

Steadfast

GROUP NOTES

Steadfast

GROUP NOTES

Steadfast

1 PETER 2

Steadfast

READ 1 PETER 2

WHAT DOES THIS SAY?

Write a 2–3 sentence summary of this passage.

Who? What? Where? When?

List any repeated words or phrases.

List any transitional words.

Steadfast

1 PETER 2 NOTES

WHAT DOES THIS SAY ABOUT GOD?

What characteristics of God do you see in this passage?

WHAT DOES THIS MEAN?

Look up the following words in the dictionary and write out their definitions:

Pure:

Priesthood:

_____:

_____:

Steadfast

CROSS-REFERENCES

Mark 12:1–12:

Acts 4:5–12:

Psalm 23:

_____:

_____:

STARTER QUESTIONS

DISCUSSION: How do these Old Testament cross-references help further explain Peter's message in this chapter?

Isaiah 28:16:

Psalm 118:

Isaiah 8:11–15:

Exodus 19:1–6:

Steadfast

How does Peter describe the family of God?

DISCUSSION: Read Leviticus 19:9–18. What does it look like to live out 1 Peter 2:16–17?

Consult a cultural commentary to learn more about ancient slavery. How does the cultural context help you better understand the call of this passage?

DISCUSSION: Read Isaiah 53:1–12. Why are we able to submit to our Just Judge, Good Shepherd, and Suffering Savior?

Steadfast

1 PETER 2 NOTES

Steadfast

1 PETER 2 NOTES

Steadfast

HOW SHOULD I RESPOND?

How is God steadfast in this chapter? How does this help you remain steadfast in faith?

Write a prayer of thanksgiving for who He is.

Because God is:

    I can:

Steadfast

TEACHING NOTES

Steadfast

TEACHING NOTES

Steadfast

GROUP NOTES

Steadfast

GROUP NOTES

Steadfast

1 PETER 3

Steadfast

READ 1 PETER 3

WHAT DOES THIS SAY?

Write a 2–3 sentence summary of this passage.

Who? What? Where? When?

List any repeated words or phrases.

List any transitional words.

Steadfast

WHAT DOES THIS SAY ABOUT GOD?

What characteristics of God do you see in this passage?

WHAT DOES THIS MEAN?

Look up the following words in the dictionary and write out their definitions:

Humility:

Zealous:

_____:

_____:

Steadfast

CROSS-REFERENCES

John 15:18–16:4:

Romans 6:1–14:

_____:

_____:

_____:

STARTER QUESTIONS

What transitional word/phrase starts this chapter? How does that help us as we begin interpreting this passage?

DISCUSSION: Consult a cultural commentary to learn more about ancient marriage and roles of women. How does the cultural context help you better understand the call of this passage?

Steadfast

How does Peter describe our witness?

DISCUSSION: Read Psalm 34. What parallels do you see in this passage and 1 Peter 3?

DISCUSSION: What does baptism represent? How does it reflect what Peter is asking us to do in this passage?

Steadfast

1 PETER 3 NOTES

Steadfast

1 PETER 3 NOTES

Steadfast

HOW SHOULD I RESPOND?

How is God steadfast in this chapter? How does this help you remain steadfast in faith?

Write a prayer of thanksgiving for who He is.

Because God is:

     I can:

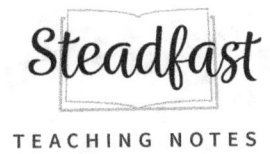

Steadfast

TEACHING NOTES

Steadfast

TEACHING NOTES

Steadfast

GROUP NOTES

Steadfast

GROUP NOTES

Steadfast

1 PETER 4

Steadfast

1 PETER 4 NOTES

READ 1 PETER 4

WHAT DOES THIS SAY?

Write a 2–3 sentence summary of this passage.

Who? What? Where? When?

List any repeated words or phrases.

List any transitional words.

Steadfast

1 PETER 4 NOTES

WHAT DOES THIS SAY ABOUT GOD?

What characteristics of God do you see in this passage?

WHAT DOES THIS MEAN?

Look up the following words in the dictionary and write out their definitions:

Faithful:

Sober:

_____:

_____:

Steadfast

CROSS-REFERENCES

Romans 12:1–21:

Proverbs 11:31:

_____:

_____:

_____:

STARTER QUESTIONS

Write out v. 1. Why is this truth an important set up for the rest of the chapter?

DISCUSSION: How do these Old Testament cross-references help further explain Peter's message in this chapter?

Jeremiah 25:29–38:

Steadfast

Daniel 12:1–2:

Jeremiah 6:27–30:

Zechariah 13:7–9:

How does Peter describe the actions of the Gentiles?

DISCUSSION: What actions mark the life of a Christian?

DISCUSSION: According to v. 19, how are we able to live faithfully even in the midst of suffering? What does this practically look like?

Steadfast

1 PETER 4 NOTES

Steadfast

1 PETER 4 NOTES

Steadfast

HOW SHOULD I RESPOND?

How is God steadfast in this chapter? How does this help you remain steadfast in faith?

Write a prayer of thanksgiving for who He is.

Because God is:

      I can:

Steadfast

TEACHING NOTES

Steadfast

TEACHING NOTES

Steadfast

GROUP NOTES

Steadfast

GROUP NOTES

Steadfast

1 PETER 5

Steadfast

READ 1 PETER 5

WHAT DOES THIS SAY?

Write a 2–3 sentence summary of this passage.

Who? What? Where? When?

List any repeated words or phrases.

List any transitional words.

Steadfast

WHAT DOES THIS SAY ABOUT GOD?

What characteristics of God do you see in this passage?

WHAT DOES THIS MEAN?

Look up the following words in the dictionary and write out their definitions:

Humility:

Shepherd:

_____:

_____:

Steadfast

CROSS-REFERENCES

John 10:1–18:

Ezekiel 34:1–31:

_____ :

_____ :

STARTER QUESTIONS

What two ways does Peter describe himself in v. 1? Think back over Peter's history. Where in Scripture do we see evidence of these?

DISCUSSION: While vv. 1–4 are specifically addressed to church elders, what can we learn about the way in which we should lead and relate to one another?

Steadfast

DISCUSSION: What is our enemy doing? Think back over Peter's life. Where do you see the enemy doing this to him?

DISCUSSION: How do we resist the enemy?

What will God ultimately do after all suffering? How does He do this even now?

What final call does Peter give in v. 12?

Think back over all of 1 Peter. How can you be steadfast in faith, even in the midst of hardship and trials?

DISCUSSION: What did you learn about God through 1 Peter?

Steadfast

1 PETER 5 NOTES

Steadfast

1 PETER 5 NOTES

Steadfast

HOW SHOULD I RESPOND?

How is God steadfast in this chapter? How does this help you remain steadfast in faith?

Write a prayer of thanksgiving for who He is.

Because God is:

    I can:

Steadfast

TEACHING NOTES

Steadfast

TEACHING NOTES

Steadfast

GROUP NOTES

Steadfast

GROUP NOTES

Steadfast

2 PETER 1

Steadfast

2 PETER 1 NOTES

READ 2 PETER 1

WHAT DOES THIS SAY?

Write a 2–3 sentence summary of this passage.

Who? What? Where? When?

List any repeated words or phrases.

List any transitional words.

Steadfast

WHAT DOES THIS SAY ABOUT GOD?

What characteristics of God do you see in this passage?

WHAT DOES THIS MEAN?

Look up the following words in the dictionary and write out their definitions:

Knowledge:

Promise:

_____:

_____:

Steadfast

2 PETER 1 NOTES

CROSS-REFERENCES

Hebrews 2:1:

Mark 9:2–13:

_____:

_____:

STARTER QUESTIONS

What role does knowledge play in our faith according to this passage?

What two words are used to describe the promises of God?

DISCUSSION: What are the virtues of faith listed in vv. 5–7? How do these virtues help us?

Why did Peter say he wrote this final letter?

Steadfast

DISCUSSION: How does Peter prove that he is not just another false prophet?

How did God give and preserve His Word?

DISCUSSION: What do these cross-references teach us about God's Word?

Isaiah 55:8–11:

Psalm 19:7–11:

Psalm 119:9:

Isaiah 40:8:

Hebrews 4:12:

2 Timothy 3:16–17:

Steadfast

2 PETER 1 NOTES

Steadfast

2 PETER 1 NOTES

Steadfast

HOW SHOULD I RESPOND?

How is God steadfast in this chapter? How does this help you remain steadfast in faith?

Write a prayer of thanksgiving for who He is.

Because God is:

    I can:

Steadfast

TEACHING NOTES

Steadfast

TEACHING NOTES

Steadfast

GROUP NOTES

Steadfast

GROUP NOTES

Steadfast

2 PETER 2

Steadfast

READ 2 PETER 2

WHAT DOES THIS SAY?

Write a 2–3 sentence summary of this passage.

Who? What? Where? When?

List any repeated words or phrases.

List any transitional words.

Steadfast

WHAT DOES THIS SAY ABOUT GOD?

What characteristics of God do you see in this passage?

WHAT DOES THIS MEAN?

Look up the following words in the dictionary and write out their definitions:

False:

Blasphemy:

_____:

_____:

Steadfast

CROSS-REFERENCES

2 Timothy 3:1–7:

Ezekiel 13:1–23:

_____:

_____:

STARTER QUESTIONS

In contrast to the true Word of God, how does Peter describe false prophets?

What will God do to false prophets?

Steadfast

Peter mentions several stories from the Old Testament. How does each prove God's faithful and just judgment?

Genesis 6:1–8:22:

Genesis 19:1–29:

Numbers 22:1–41:

DISCUSSION: How does knowledge help us discern false teachings from the truth of God's Word?

Steadfast

2 PETER 2 NOTES

Steadfast

2 PETER 2 NOTES

Steadfast

2 PETER 2 NOTES

HOW SHOULD I RESPOND?

How is God steadfast in this chapter? How does this help you remain steadfast in faith?

Write a prayer of thanksgiving for who He is.

Because God is:

      I can:

Steadfast

TEACHING NOTES

Steadfast

TEACHING NOTES

Steadfast

GROUP NOTES

Steadfast

GROUP NOTES

Steadfast

2 PETER 3

Steadfast

READ 2 PETER 3

WHAT DOES THIS SAY?

Write a 2–3 sentence summary of this passage.

Who? What? Where? When?

List any repeated words or phrases.

List any transitional words.

Steadfast

WHAT DOES THIS SAY ABOUT GOD?

What characteristics of God do you see in this passage?

WHAT DOES THIS MEAN?

Look up the following words in the dictionary and write out their definitions:

Patient:

Diligent:

Scoffers:

_____:

Steadfast

CROSS-REFERENCES

Matthew 24:36–48:

Genesis 1:1-2; 7:1-24:

_____:

_____:

STARTER QUESTIONS

What objection do the scoffers make against God?

How does Peter respond to their objections?

DISCUSSION: What does this tell us about our own responses in encounters with scoffers?

Steadfast

How do these verses support what Peter says is to come?

Psalm 50:1–6:

Romans 8:18–30:

Hebrews 12:18–29:

Revelation 21:1–8:

DISCUSSION: Knowing God will be faithful to do as He has promised, how should we live?

DISCUSSION: Think back over the entire study. What do you now know about God? How does that help you remain stable and steadfast in your faith?

Steadfast

2 PETER 3 NOTES

Steadfast

2 PETER 3 NOTES

Steadfast

HOW SHOULD I RESPOND?

How is God steadfast in this chapter? How does this help you remain steadfast in faith?

Write a prayer of thanksgiving for who He is.

Because God is:

    I can:

Steadfast

TEACHING NOTES

Steadfast

TEACHING NOTES

Steadfast

GROUP NOTES

Steadfast

GROUP NOTES

Steadfast

ADDITIONAL NOTES

Steadfast

ADDITIONAL NOTES

Steadfast

ADDITIONAL NOTES

Steadfast

ADDITIONAL NOTES

feasting at the table

For as long as I can remember I have loved chocolate and peanut butter together. I mean, is there a better flavor combination? And throw in some crispy rice cereal? Even better! Over the years I have tweaked and, dare I say, perfected this recipe with love and careful deliberateness. The final product ends up looking like giant rocks of yumminess, which is why my family affectionately dubbed them "Chocolate Peanut Butter Boulders". We love these crispy, crunchy, peanut buttery, chocolate-covered treats.

As a mom to a diabetic, I'm constantly looking for ways to create or modify our favorite treats to make them less sugary and more nutritiously balanced in their ingredients. Which, let's face it, is good for everyone! Opting for a peanut butter labeled "natural" typically means you'll get less sugar and more protein in each bite. While I wouldn't necessarily call them "healthy", these treats are certainly easier to enjoy without the worry of breaking the sugar bank!

Using dark chocolate brings a perfect balance and smooth finish that isn't overly sweet, and it also allows the peanut butter flavor to shine. My personal preference is to buy unsalted peanut butter and then add my own salt. So if you use salted peanut butter, be sure to omit the salt in the recipe. You can also use regular peanut butter, but your final product will be much sweeter. I'm a fan of dark chocolate (fun fact: I don't like milk chocolate at all!), but feel free to use semi-sweet chocolate if you prefer.

Don't get me wrong: I love sugar. But every now and then, it's nice to have a treat that's somewhat guilt-free yet still full of flavor. Give 'em a try! As always, happy feasting!

ERIN'S CHOCOLATE PEANUT BUTTER BOULDERS

Time: 3–4 hours
Yield: About 3 dozen

INGREDIENTS
16 ounces natural peanut butter (just peanuts – no other ingredients)
1 teaspoon kosher salt
1 cup powdered sugar
4 tablespoons unsalted butter, room temperature
1 teaspoon vanilla
4 cups crispy rice cereal
10 ounces dark chocolate chips
3 teaspoons of coconut oil or vegetable shortening

INSTRUCTIONS
1. In a large bowl, add the peanut butter (and oil from the jar) and salt. Using a hand mixer, mix on medium speed until smooth.
2. Add in the powdered sugar, butter, and vanilla. Mix again on medium until smooth.
3. Add the crispy rice cereal and stir with a large spoon or spatula until combined.
4. Line a baking sheet with foil or parchment paper. Using a tablespoon cookie scoop, firmly pack the scoop with dough and spoon it onto the sheet. Alternatively, you can use your hands to form balls. You will want firmly packed boulders, otherwise they will fall apart when dipping.
5. Refrigerate for at least an hour.
6. When ready to dip, melt the chocolate chips and coconut oil (or vegetable shortening) over a double boiler on the stove until smooth. If using a microwave, microwave in 30 second increments, stirring each time until melted and smooth.
7. Insert a skewer or toothpick into the chilled boulder and dip in the chocolate, covering the bottom and sides. Place it back on the backing sheet and repeat with the remaining boulders.
8. Chill the boulders one more time for about two hours or until the chocolate is set. Enjoy!

about Erin

ERIN H. WARREN is passionate about equipping and encouraging women to discover God's truths for themselves. She is the author of *Feasting on Truth: Savor the Life-giving Word of God* and *Everyday Prayers for Faith: Finding Confidence in God No Matter What*. She leads and teaches Bible study through her ministry Feasting on Truth and has published several Bible studies. She and her husband, Kris, have three littles (who aren't so little anymore), and they live in Central Florida. She loves a house full of people and a table full of food and hopes tacos never go out of style. You can find more information about Feasting on Truth on her website: FeastingOnTruth.com. You can also connect with her on Instagram: @erinhwarren and @feastingontruth and YouTube: www.youtube.com/c/erinhwarren.

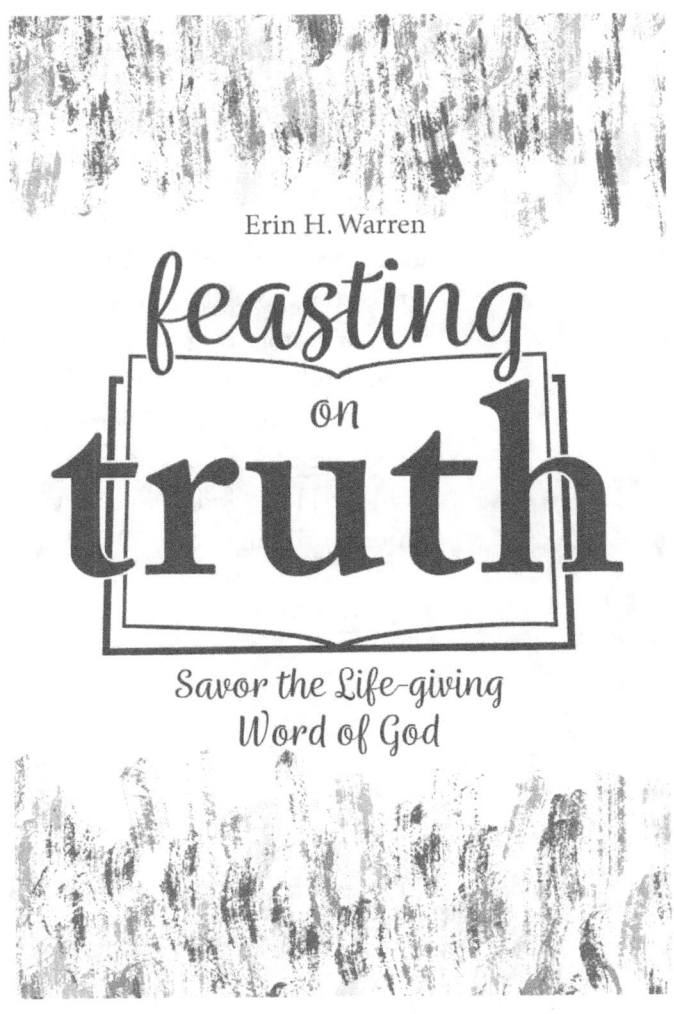

Erin H. Warren

feasting on truth

Savor the Life-giving
Word of God

FEASTING ON TRUTH

SAVOR THE LIFE-GIVING WORD OF GOD

We know reading the Bible is important, but sometimes it's hard to know where to start or how to make sense of these ancient words. For years, Erin Warren struggled to do the same. Then she found a simple approach that changed everything.

As she shares her own story, Erin guides the reader to a deeper understanding of why we need to study Scripture and how to do it. Her desire is to encourage and equip women to discover God's truths for themselves.

The word *feast* is rooted in abundance. That is what awaits us in the pages of Scripture: a table laid out before us, not only for our essential nourishment, but for our enjoyment.

FeastingOnTruth.com/Books

TO DWELL IN OUR MIDST

A STUDY OF THE TABERNACLE AND HOW IT POINTS US TO JESUS

Why study this ancient tent? What does knowing about the Tabernacle have to do with our faith on this side of the cross? Everything. This tent is not merely ritual or history or good information—it's essential to understanding our salvation. Our detailed and deliberate God gave us the Tabernacle because one day, He would give us Jesus. It's an invitation into a relationship with our Holy God. Discover God's plan to dwell in our midst through Jesus Christ.

FeastingOnTruth.com/Dwell

STORIES FROM THE WILDERNESS

A STUDY OF THE ISRAELITES' JOURNEY FROM EGYPT TO THE PROMISED LAND

The wilderness. It is a place that feels hard, empty, lifeless, and pathless, and it often leaves us with questions about who God is. But where we see a place that is worthless, confusing, and chaotic, God sees a place to display His power. Time and time again throughout Scripture, God takes the worthless, seemingly wasteful, confusing, chaotic, and empty places and uses them as a backdrop to prove His character, draw us in, and display His glory.

FeastingOnTruth.com/Wilderness

WAY MAKER

AN ADVENT STUDY THROUGH THE BOOK OF HEBREWS

Jesus' coming was more than giving us forgiveness of sins or to part the way before us. He came to part the divide between God and us, between us and heaven. Jesus is the One who made a way to a restored relationship with God. No other book gives us a more comprehensive view of Jesus as our Way Maker than the book of Hebrews.

FeastingOnTruth.com/WayMaker

LIGHT & LIFE

AN INDUCTIVE STUDY ON PSALM 119

We hear it all the time: we need to read the Bible every day. But why is it so important that we know, understand, and apply this ancient book to our lives today? What's in it for us? In Psalm 119, we see over and over that God's Word brings life, and it's a light to guide us. If we truly knew the power the Word of God has in our lives, we wouldn't be able to put it down.

FeastingOnTruth.com/LightAndLife

BY HIS GRACE FOR HIS GLORY

AN INDUCTIVE STUDY ON THE BOOK OF ROMANS

Romans is foundational yet deep. It's hard to understand yet simple. It is an incredibly powerful book that has been changing lives for centuries, and the truths in these sixteen chapters have the power to change our faith too. There are many familiar verses in Romans, and we associate this book with evangelism. But it is so much more! Discover what it looks like to live by His grace for His glory.

FeastingOnTruth.com/Romans

UNEXPECTED SAVIOR

AN INDUCTIVE STUDY ON THE GOSPEL OF MARK

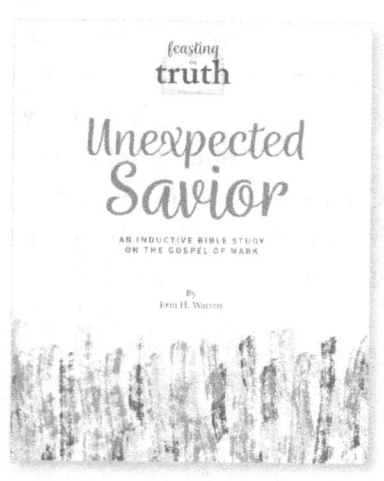

The Gospel of Mark challenges the expected ideal of the Messiah—not a conquering king or a wish-granting genie, but rather a man of sorrows and a suffering servant. This short yet impactful account of Jesus' life reveals the character of the One who came to save us. Jesus mourned the brokenness around Him: the sickness, the pain, the hardness of heart. He grew angry at the sin of those who led His sheep astray. He was the One who came not to be served, but to serve. He came to prove the faithfulness of God and provide unshakable hope as we walk through hardships.

FeastingOnTruth.com/Mark

www.ingramcontent.com/pod-product-compliance
Lightning Source LLC
Chambersburg PA
CBHW081332120626
46546CB00011B/3309